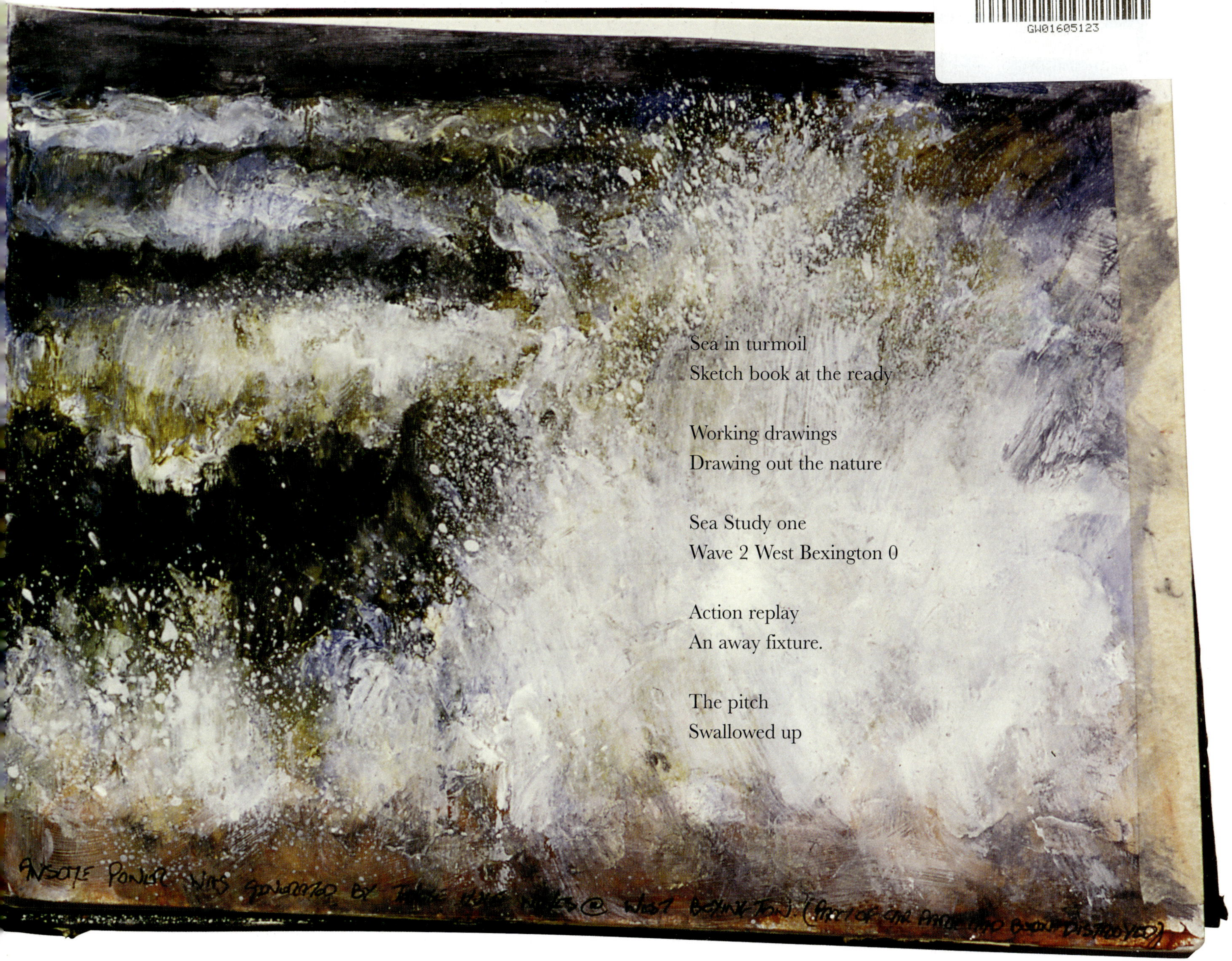

Sea in turmoil
Sketch book at the ready

Working drawings
Drawing out the nature

Sea Study one
Wave 2 West Bexington 0

Action replay
An away fixture.

The pitch
Swallowed up

Coastlines – *Chasing the Light*

PAINTINGS

by Michael J Chappell

POEMS

by James Crowden

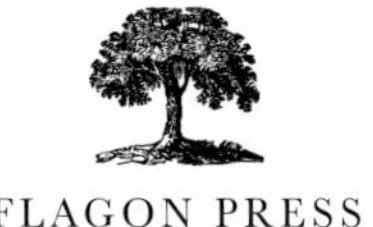

FLAGON PRESS

First published 2008
By Flagon Press
Whitelackington
Designed by Andrew Crane
Printed in Milborne Port by Remous Ltd

Typeset in Monotype Baskerville

ISBN 978-0-9557073-5-3

Front cover:

East Cliff – West Bay
Mixed media with collage
168 x 92cm

This book is dedicated

to my wife Janice for her love, support and encouragement

which has seen me through my 'black dog' days.

MICHAEL J CHAPPELL

MICHAEL J CHAPPELL – *Artistic Visionary*

A visionary, according to the Oxford English Dictionary, is someone with imaginative insight, statesmanlike foresight and sagacity in planning - MICHAEL J CHAPPELL has all of these qualities both as a man and as an artist. Michael is my friend and I am proud to be his. We both arrived in Dorset around the same time – last century!

Born in Finedon, a small village in Northamptonshire, Michael left school at 15 with a dream of going to university and a thirst to study art. Coming from a close-knit but working class family, there was little chance of pursuing his dream but encouraged by his siblings, particularly his sister Ruby and her husband David, Michael continued to paint and develop his natural talent and exhibit his work locally. His career as a youth worker enabled him to teach art and use art as a therapy for young people with social problems, to express their feelings. Michael has continued to teach – he is an inspirational enabler and has the patience to encourage and empower would-be artists of all ages.

Thirty-five years passed by and Michael married Janice and they had two children, Simon and Zöe, only then did he decide to try to fulfil his early ambitions and, spurred on by his wife, he achieved a BA (hons) in Fine Art at the University of Central England. Michael has won many awards for his artistic endeavours including:

1997 Emma Jessie Phipps award in Theoretical Art Studies

1997 Whitworth Wallis Marine Painting Competition Medal Winner

2001 1st Prize in Sculpture and installation Bridport Open Art Competition

2003 2nd Prize and voted 2nd most popular exhibitor Bridport Art Open Competition

It has taken Michael ten years since graduating to have the time, and the courage, to put together a book of his work, which illustrates the development of his own very personal visual language, and to communicate this vocabulary to the viewer through this work.

Michael's paintings illuminate and breathe the local landscape and seascape of West Dorset and yet reach far beyond the representation of what he sees, and what we see too. They are windows onto a world that we can feel, touch, smell, inhale as well as see. Countryside in summer sunshine and winter rain, spring renewal and autumnal decline; seascapes that reflect the ever-changing emotions of the ocean – silent, serene, angry, tumultuous. The paintings are profound and the sketchbooks are every bit as fascinating as they chart the journey of the artist's eyes.

Coastlines is a visual hymn to all that is glorious along the Jurassic Coast and inland to a timeless and unique landscape that is Dorset.

TANYA BRUCE-LOCKHART
Friend and Trustee of Dorset Visual Arts

ARTIST'S STATEMENT

It is 10 years since I graduated from the UCE in Birmingham. I have spent that time developing a visual language that transcends a purely figurative representation of nature, in order to introduce the viewer to a new way of seeing that involves all the senses, so that my paintings can be experienced rather than just viewed. It is only now that I am happy to produce a book of my work although that does not mean my journey is complete, far from it, and over time I hope to continue to refine this language making it increasingly more communicative and expansive.

I always paint *en plein air*, mostly in the autumn and winter in all weathers so that almost by osmosis the atmospheric condition pass through me onto the canvas. My work captures a moment in time that could be almost any moment in time because each storm, each fleeting glimpse of light, each splash of sea is painted with the collective experience of hundreds of storms, hundreds of fleeting glimpses of light and thousands of splashes of the sea. My visual schema of the sea contains an image formed from a thousand images, so each seascape is not just a single seascape, but each is legion.

My influences are many and varied but first and foremost is Joan Eardley who amazingly is mostly unknown outside of Scotland. Yet those who are competent to make the judgement rightly consider her the greatest Scottish artist since McTaggart. Other contemporary artists confirming my path as much as influencing me include, Terry Setch, Len Tabner and Kurt Jackson.

Although my work is not as abstracted as Eardly's, it does contain passages that rely more on the quality of the painted mark rather than a precise visual representation, in order to convey the essence of the experience of the object or scene portrayed. This is an ever-increasing trend in my work, which is moving more and more towards an abstract painterly style as I allow my paint to virtually metamorphose into its equivalent in nature. The secret of communication is in the mark and I believe we all have a subconscious collective visual language of marks that evoke emotional responses within us, much as colour does. It is something that Betty Edwards has explored in the analogue drawings made by her students; What Jung described as a collective unconsciousness.

In my work I am trying to resolve a dichotomy between the external visual experience and this internal visual language so that just as the abstract expressionists believed, whatever goes into a painting must inevitably come out of it and in the process of time be felt and understood.

I am already planning my next book 'Landlines', in which I hope to make my painterly language even more expansive and dynamic, through the continuing development of my painting style.

MICHAEL J CHAPPELL 2008

Eype Mouth

The sea yawning -

No bedrock in sight.

Gully run

Reeds like a brook -

Whistling in the wind

Mudstone moving

The low sunshine -

A decayed path

High and dry

Old boats keeling over -

Bottoms up.

Eype mouth in winter

Mixed media
38 x 38cm

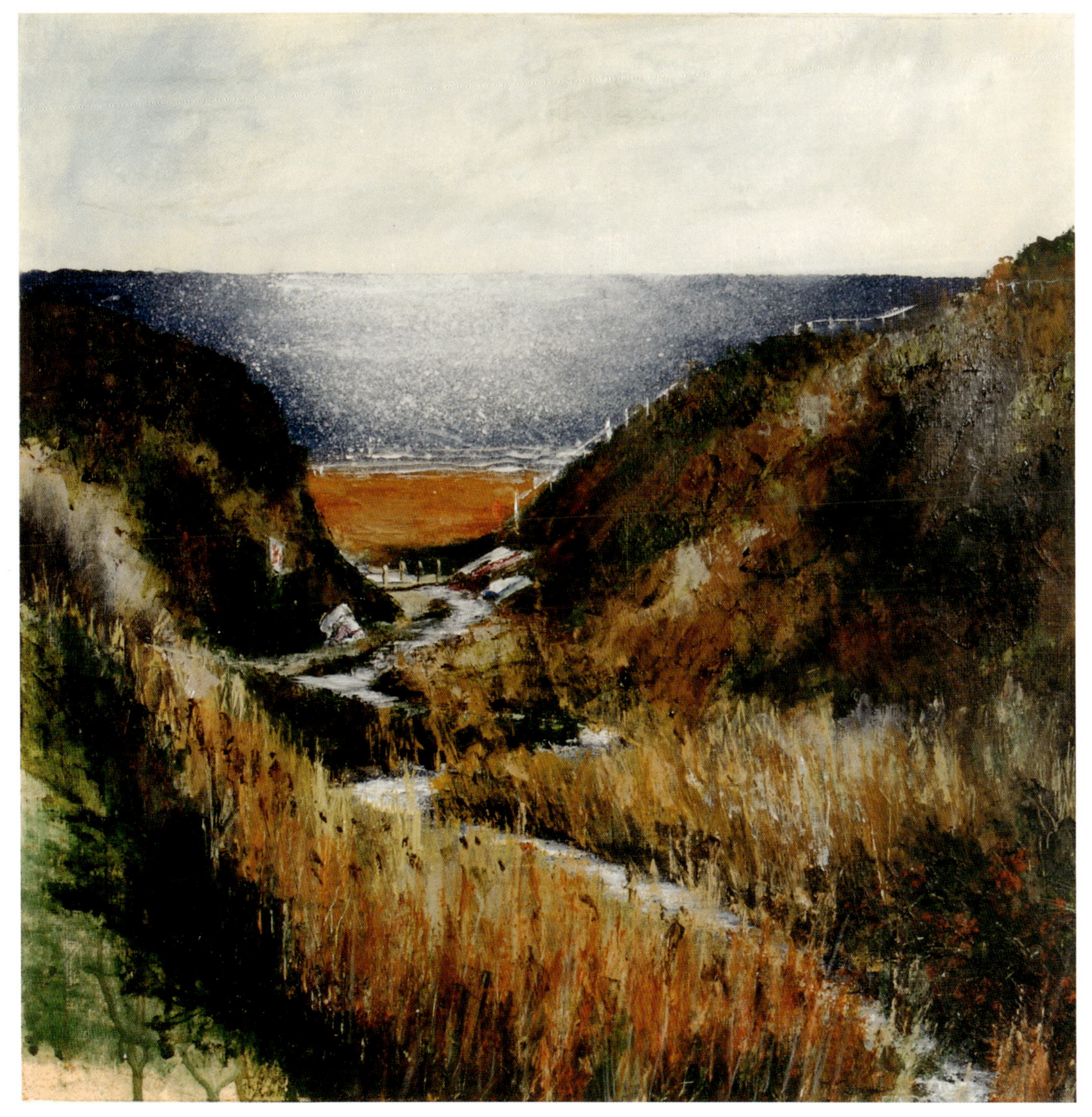

Looking east, each wave
Desultory, shadowing the coast.
Etching the cliff

Crumbling impermanence
Is welcomed back
The sea's launderette

The Jurassic Cycle,
Prewash - Heavy soil,
Colourfast - short spin, long spin

A few million years later
Fossils re-emerge fresh and clean.
Evolution - washed out.

Charmouth

As fast as I put on the paint the rain tried to wash it off again!

Mixed media
37 x 37cm

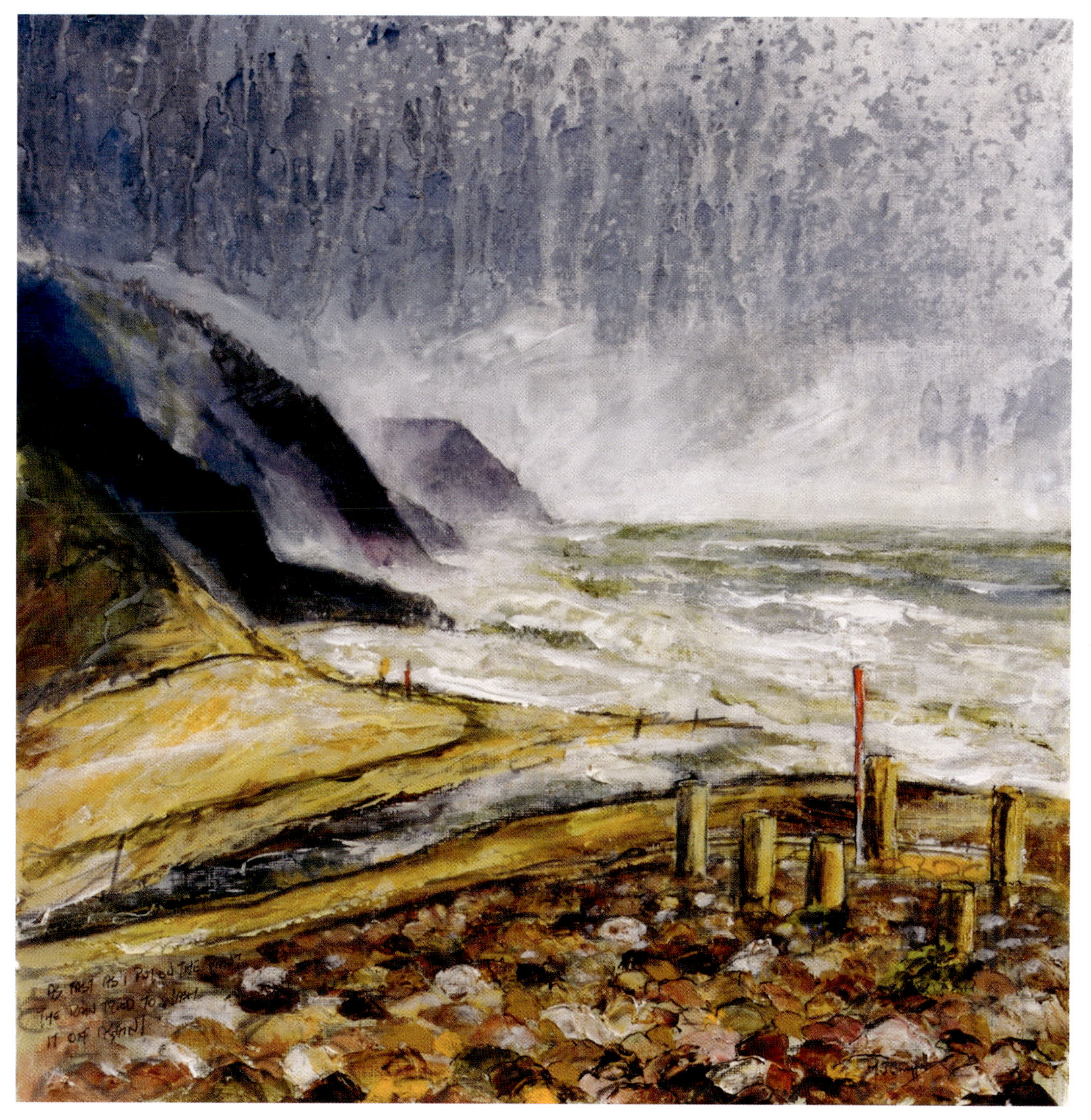
AS FAST AS I PUT ON THE PAINT
THE RAIN TRIED TO WASH
IT OFF AGAIN!

Looking down to Worbarrow Tout
Embayed, the seascape far below
Glitters, anchoring the light

Haunt of fishermen and smugglers
Public access, well in hand,
Lobster pots on the run.

An explosive situation
Old shells, unearthed
Tyneham, Arish Mell, Portland

Medium wave, long wave, short wave
The sea broadcasting on its own frequency -
Weather forecast in a grain of sand.

Worbarrow Bay

It was a steep climb, so we rested when we reached the gorse bush.

Mixed media
37.5 x 37.5cm

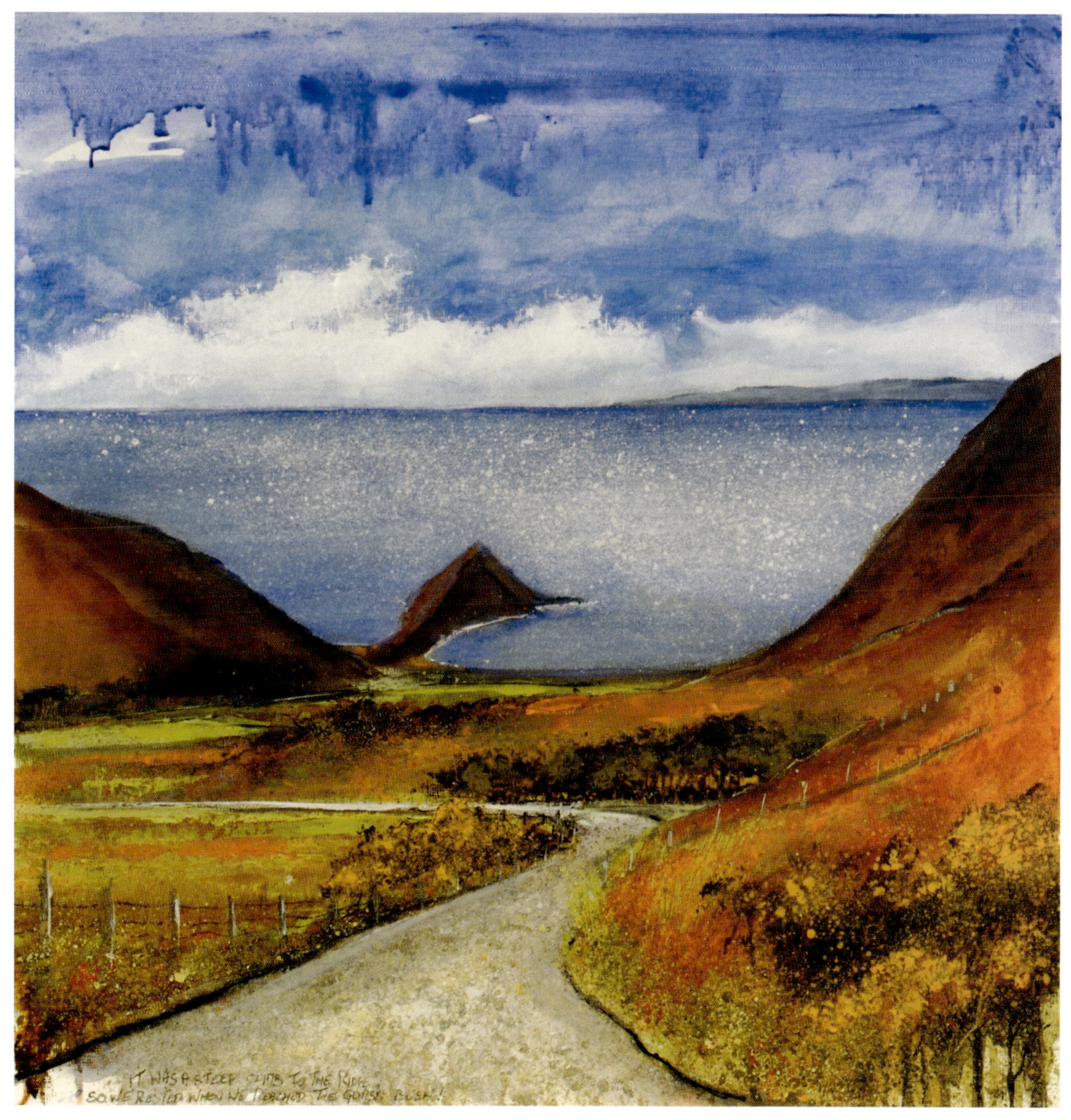
IT WAS A STEEP CLIMB TO THE RIDGE
SO WE RESTED WHEN WE REACHED THE GORSE BUSH!

The Wild West

First line of defence

Chasing the light

Gnawing the coast

The sea's eruptions

Echoing the sky

The harbour mouth.

Entrenched

With fish and chips

A sheet anchor,

The corral of rocks

Last stand - Impermanence.

Jurassic Coastline

Mixed media
38 x 38cm

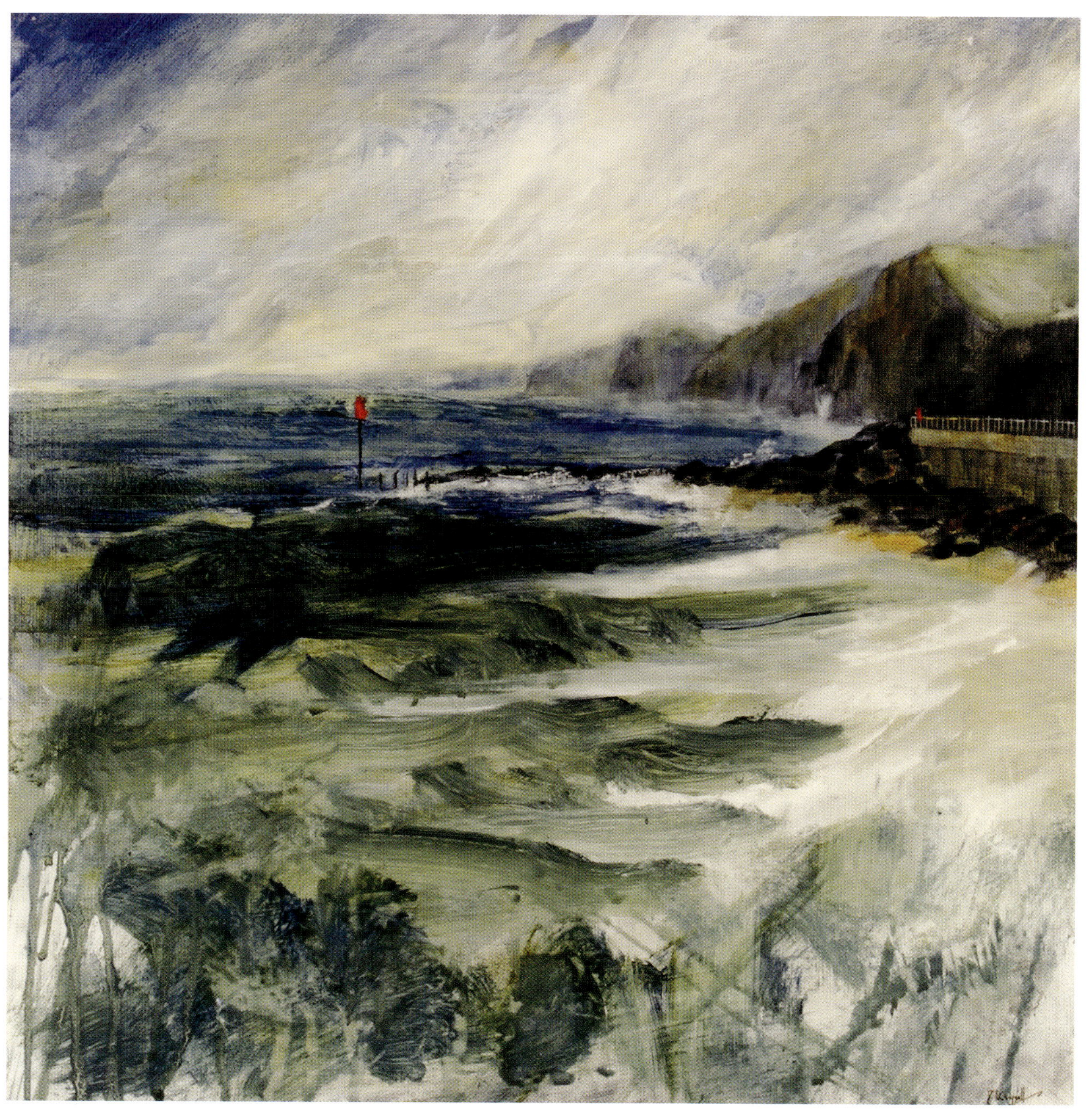

Smuggling moon,
The night sky's cape
Fair wind for France
Gulliver's travels

Brandy Vicar?
Each wave
A silver shoal
Of invisible herring

The sea's blanket pulled tight
Ankers at midnight
Muffled oars and footsteps
The silence imported, duty free.

West Bay harbour by moonlight

Mixed media
37 x 37cm

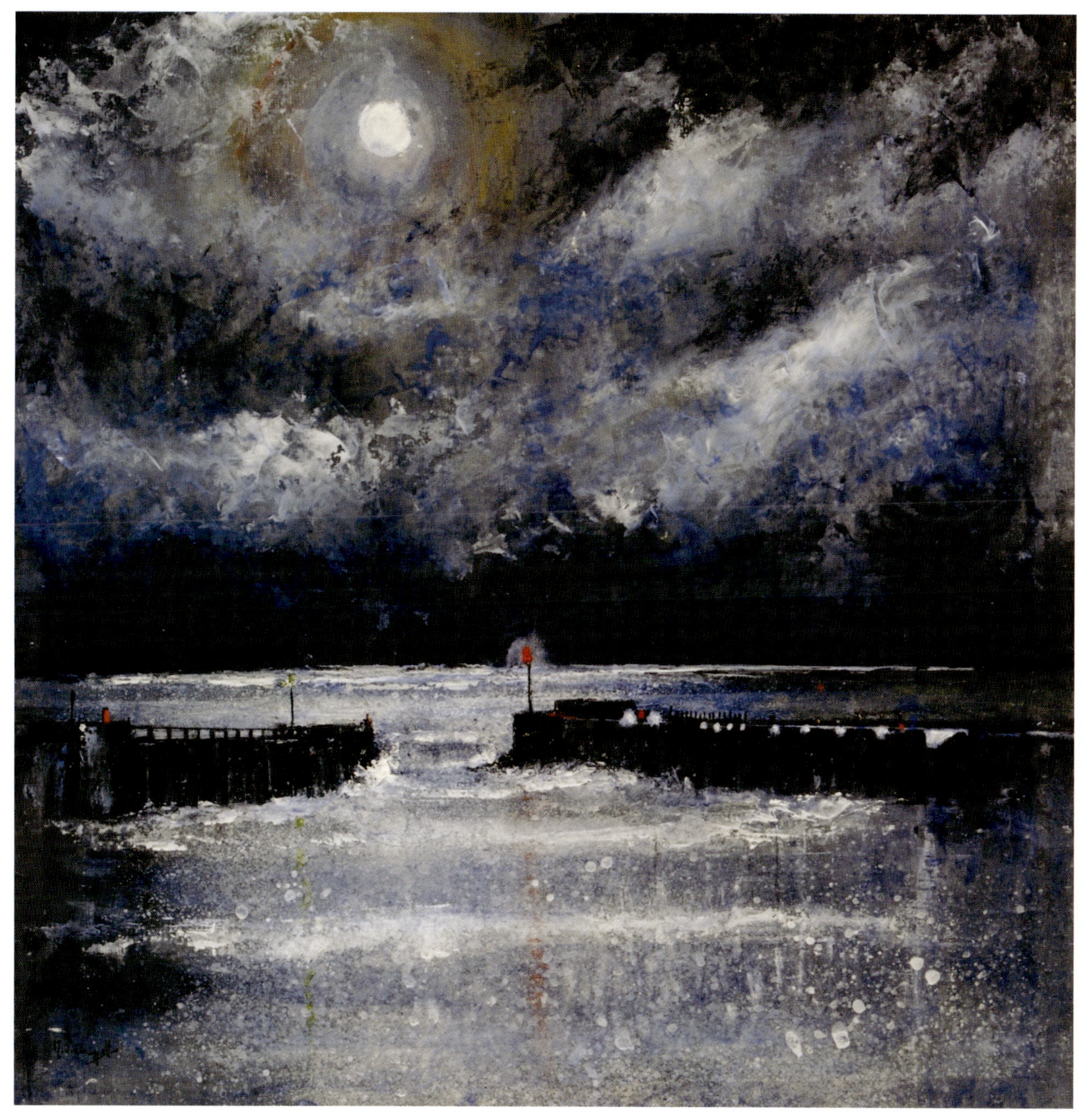

Reaching far up the Axe
On a falling tide,
Fresh on salt, mingled
Migrating routes

For ospreys and salmon
Eels and sea trout
Gourmet otters
Discreet their visiting cards

Left on the bank,
Spoilt for choice
The Yarty as well
Wetland pent up.

Quills for the abbey.
Swanning around
Gin Bottle Hole, Hope Pool
Meanders reflected.

The Axe estuary on a falling tide

Mixed media
39.5 x 38.5cm

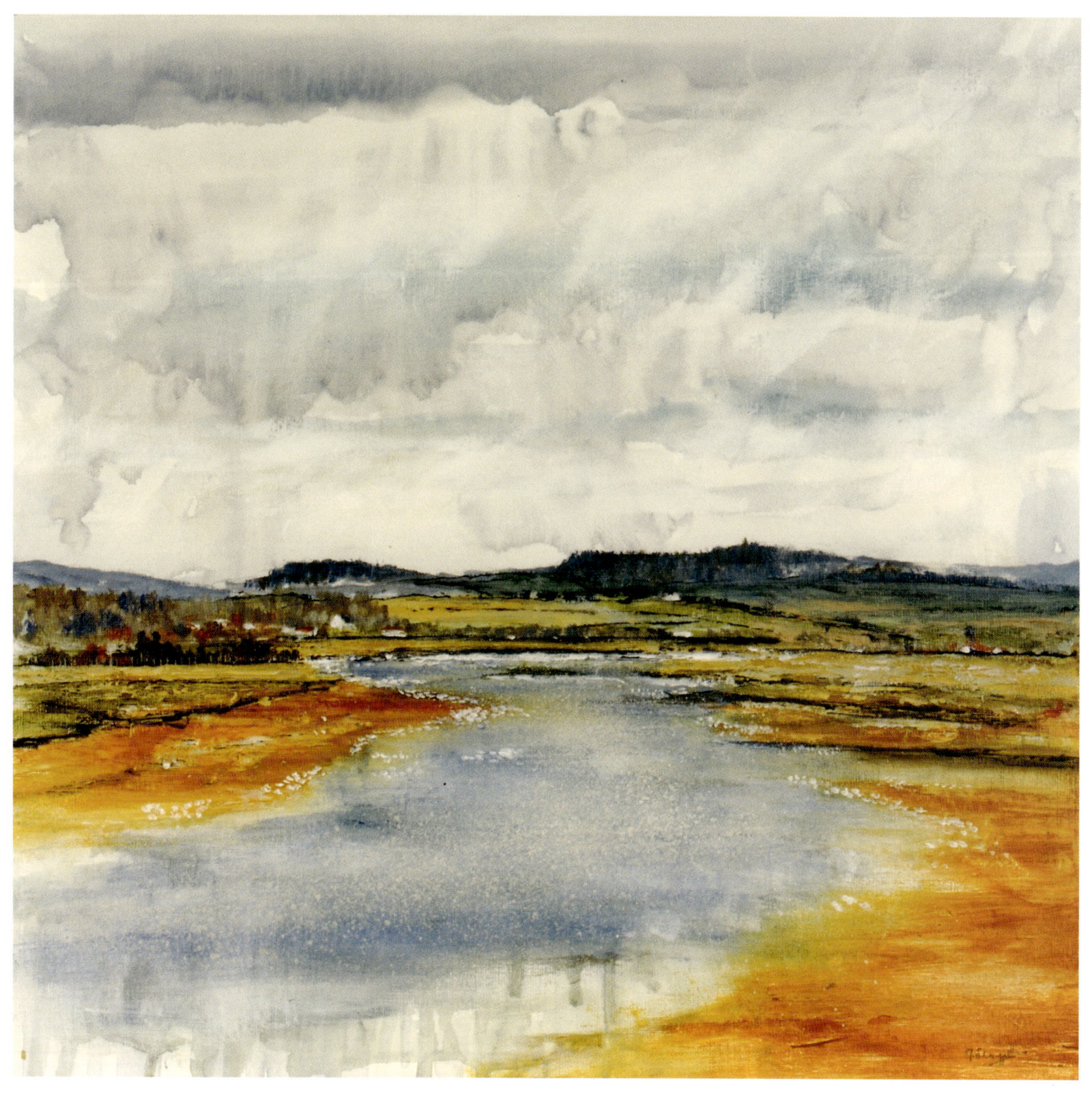

Devonshire Head

Rocks telling the time of day

High tide on ammonites

Shore thing - beachcombing

This could be Australia

Or West Coast America

That washed up feel

Drifting between ideas

Tree roots exposed

Biting the wind

Words, mere flotsam and jetsam

Cobb just out of frame.

Beneath the undercliff

The light changed every minute and the southwest wind grew stronger but only the rain eventually forced me to leave!

Mixed media
38 x 38cm

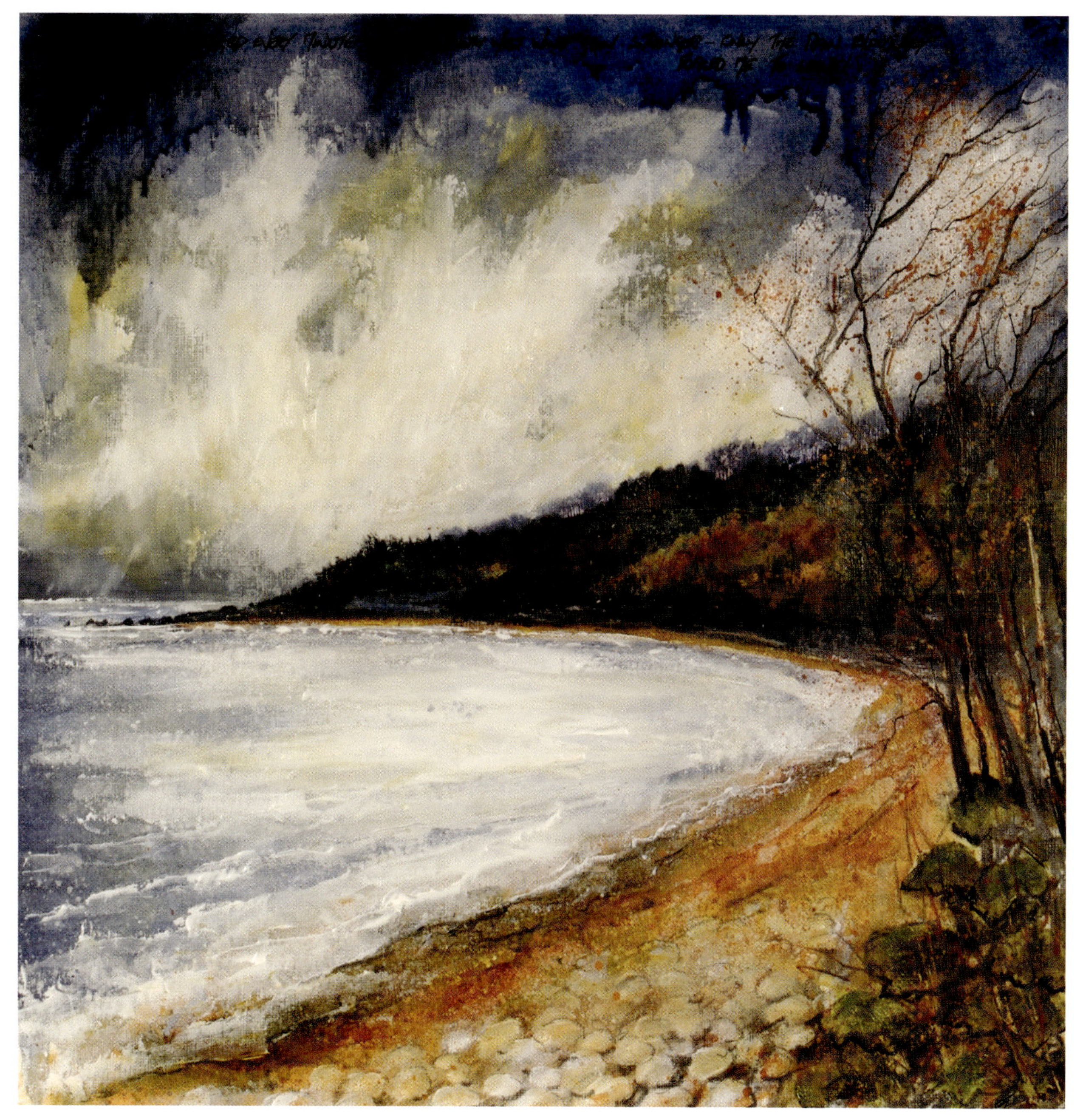

The light folded in tightly
Punctuated with fence posts

Fields catapulted
Skyward, seaward,

Landscape pulling the eye
The solstice shoot

Down House and Doghouse
Frogmore, East Ebb and Hope Corner

Eype Down encircled
On the edge

The suddenness falling away,
Dusk carried home in the game bag.

Thorncombe Beacon

Eype Down approaching dusk on the shortest day – Sounds of voices and shooting in the distance.

Mixed media
37 x 37cm

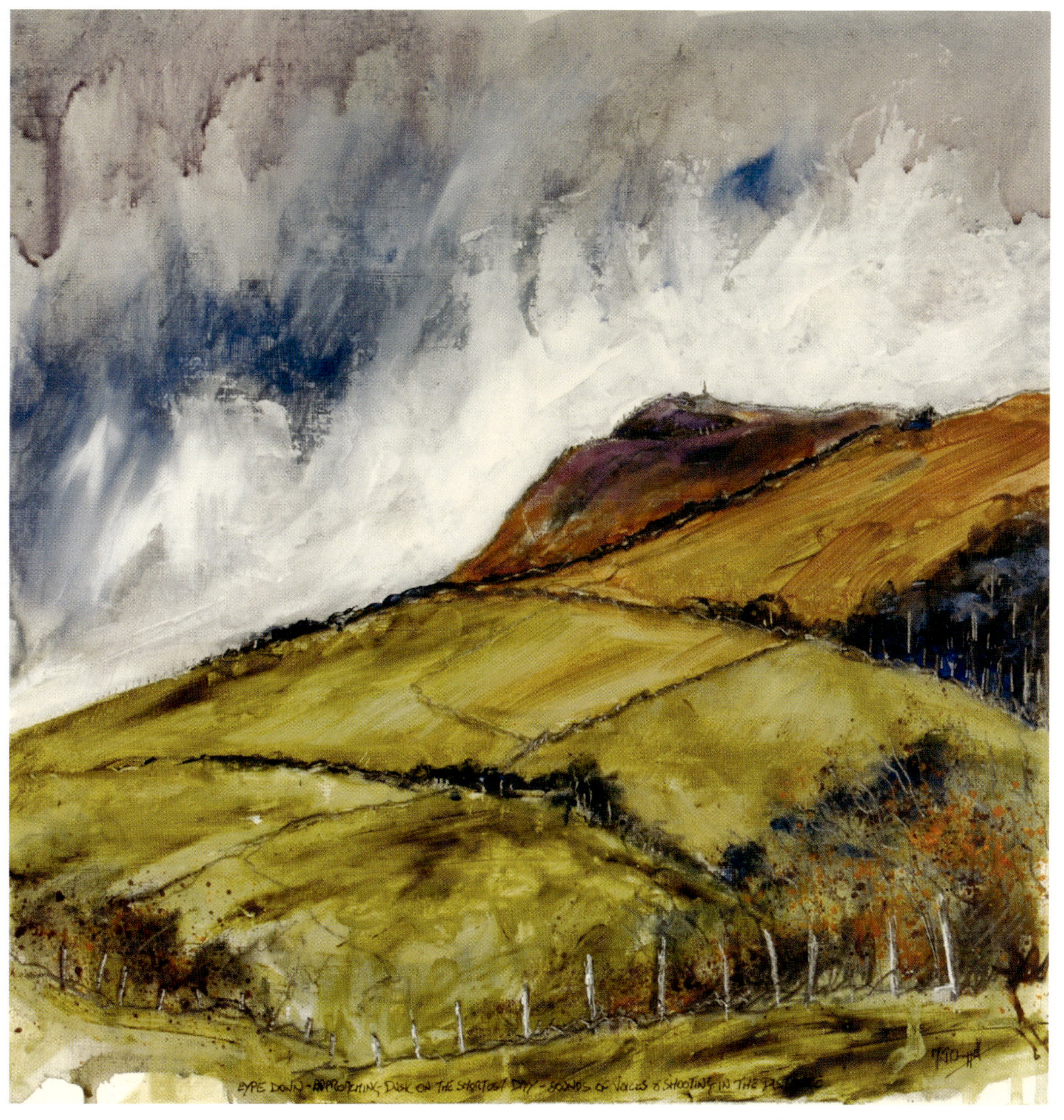
EYPE DOWN - APPROACHING DUSK ON THE SHORTEST DAY - SOUNDS OF VOICES & SHOOTING IN THE

Durlston Castle

Tilly Whim and Anvil Point

Cave rescues and tidal flurries.

To the lighthouse,

Purbeck in vogue

With dolphins and climbers

The sea's drop

Coastal architecture

Quarried out to the lip

Dancing Ledge

Round the corner

Pirouetting on the path.

Durlston Lighthouse

Sounds of Jackdaws and distant thunder of the waves below.

Mixed media
37 x 37cm

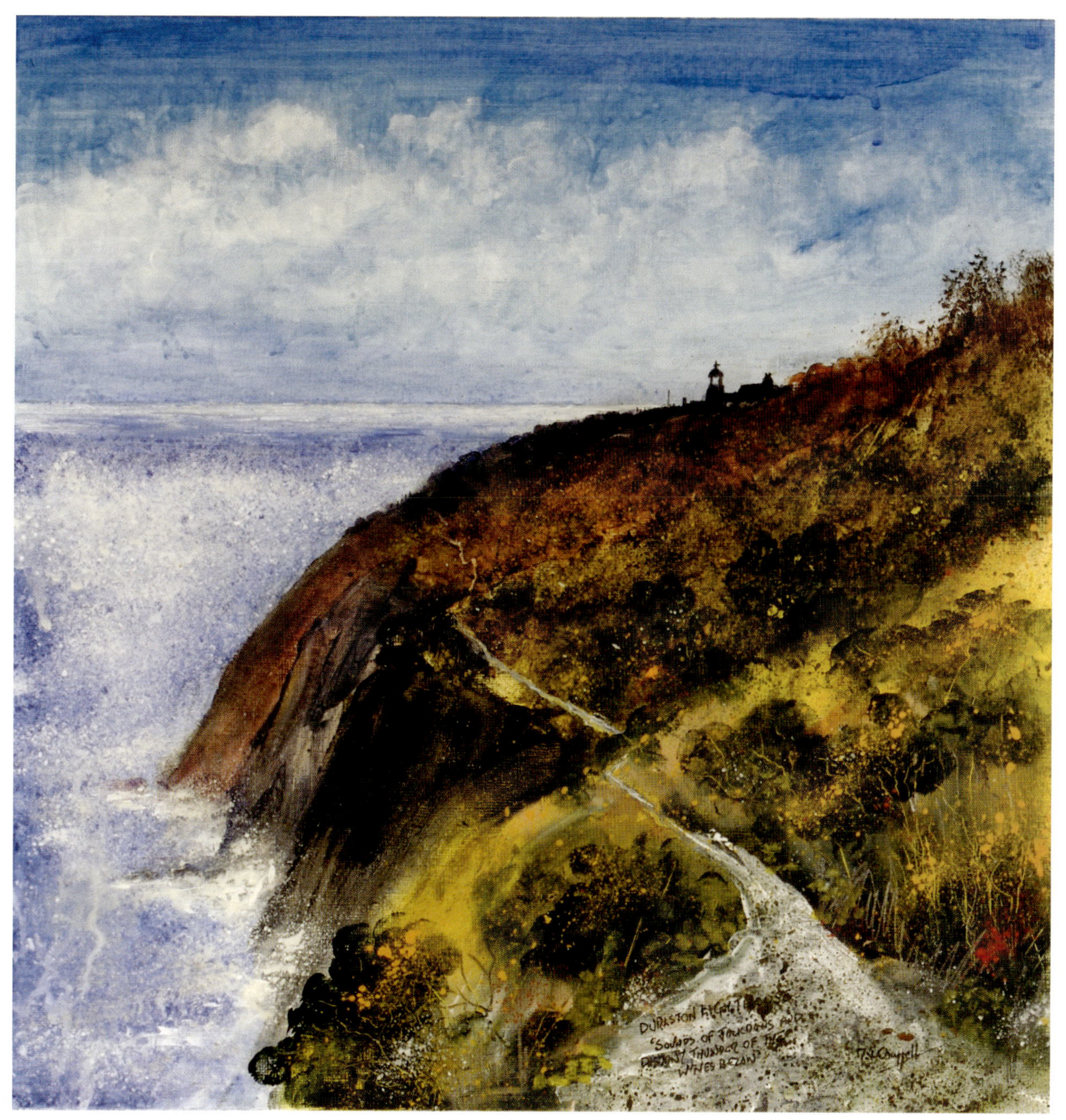

Colmer's Hill, leading mark
For farmers navigating
Into Bridport on Market Day

Symondsbury, tucked in under
With Tithe Barn and cider presses
The Mummers play, Room to manoeuvre

Introducing Colonel Spring and General Valentine
Captain Bluster and the King of Egypt
St George and the Doctor

Old Father Christmas, all battling it out
The hillside a coat of bracken
Sewn together with fallen pine needles.

Colmer's Hill

Bridport's iconic Colmer's hill painted between the showers on a cold January afternoon.

Mixed media
37 x 37cm

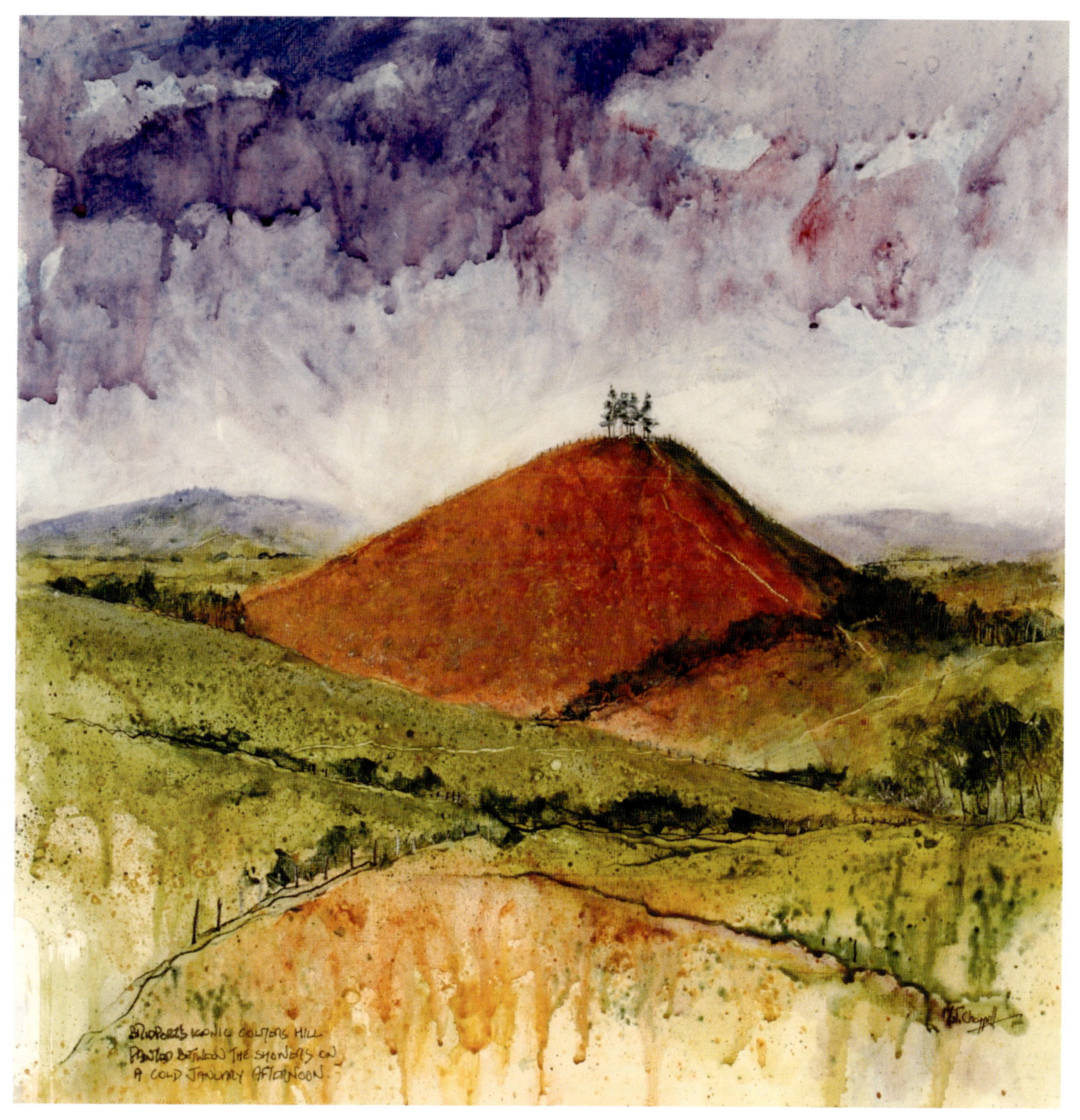
BRIDPORT'S ICONIC COLMERS HILL
PAINTED BETWEEN THE SHOWERS ON
A COLD JANUARY AFTERNOON.

Lyme Bay, sheltering
The haunt of stone boatmen
On the rocks slippage, Black Venn
The sky an addled beast
The dog watch

Shafts of light faltering
Frayed and tattered
The rocks manacled.
Scuppered. Salt –
The sea's bill of lading.

Charmouth rocks
at high tide

Sounds of seagulls, sea and spray.

Mixed media
37 x 37cm

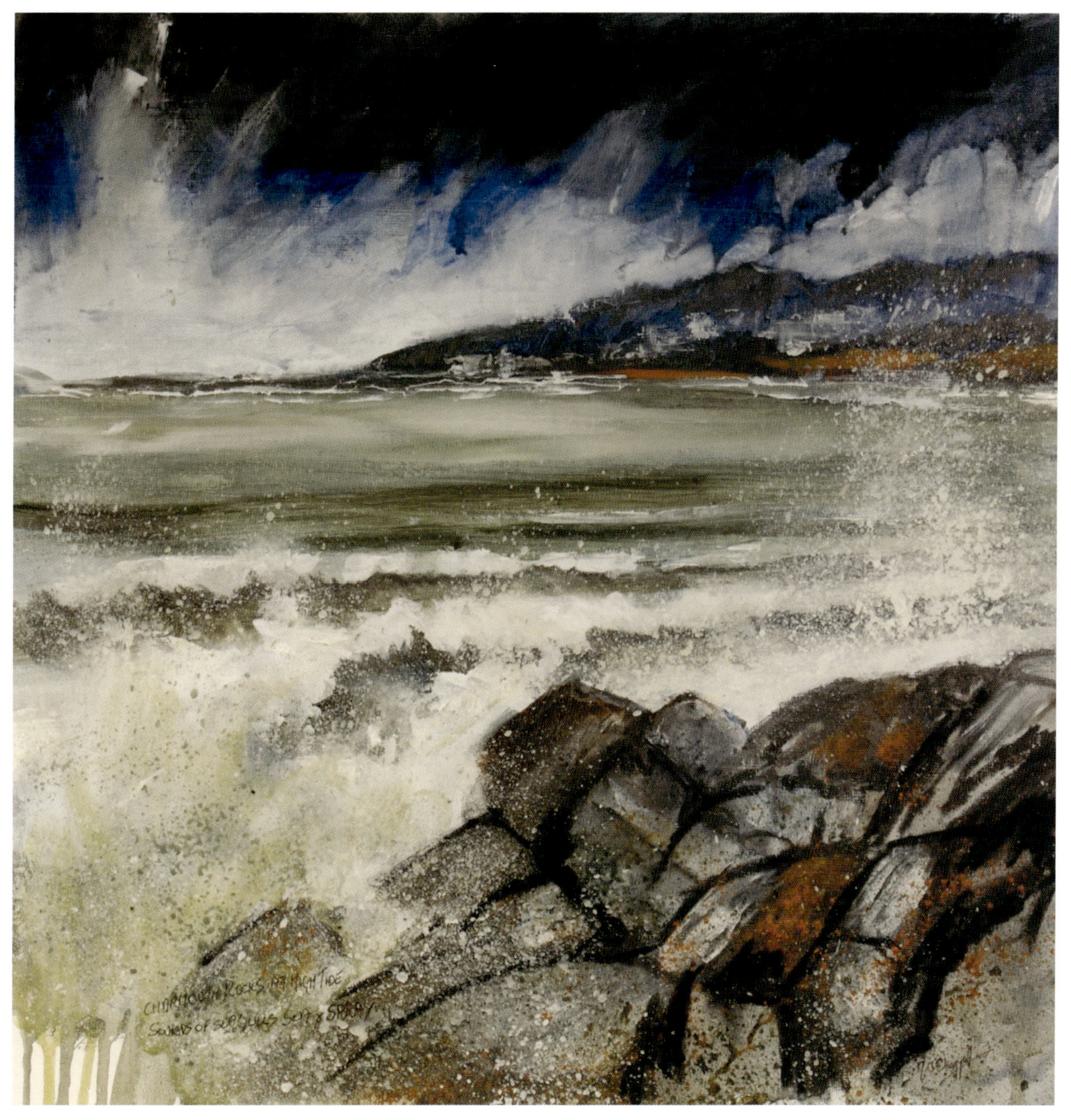
CHARMOUTH ROCKS AT HIGH TIDE

Clay Venn and seine netting

The tidal curve

Where have all the lerrets gone?

On the lawn end

Mackerel by the stone.

Passport stamped in fathoms

The beach its own hour glass

Curving towards the Bill

The whale's acre beckons.

Hive Beach

Painted on a cold February morning.

Mixed media
37 x 37cm

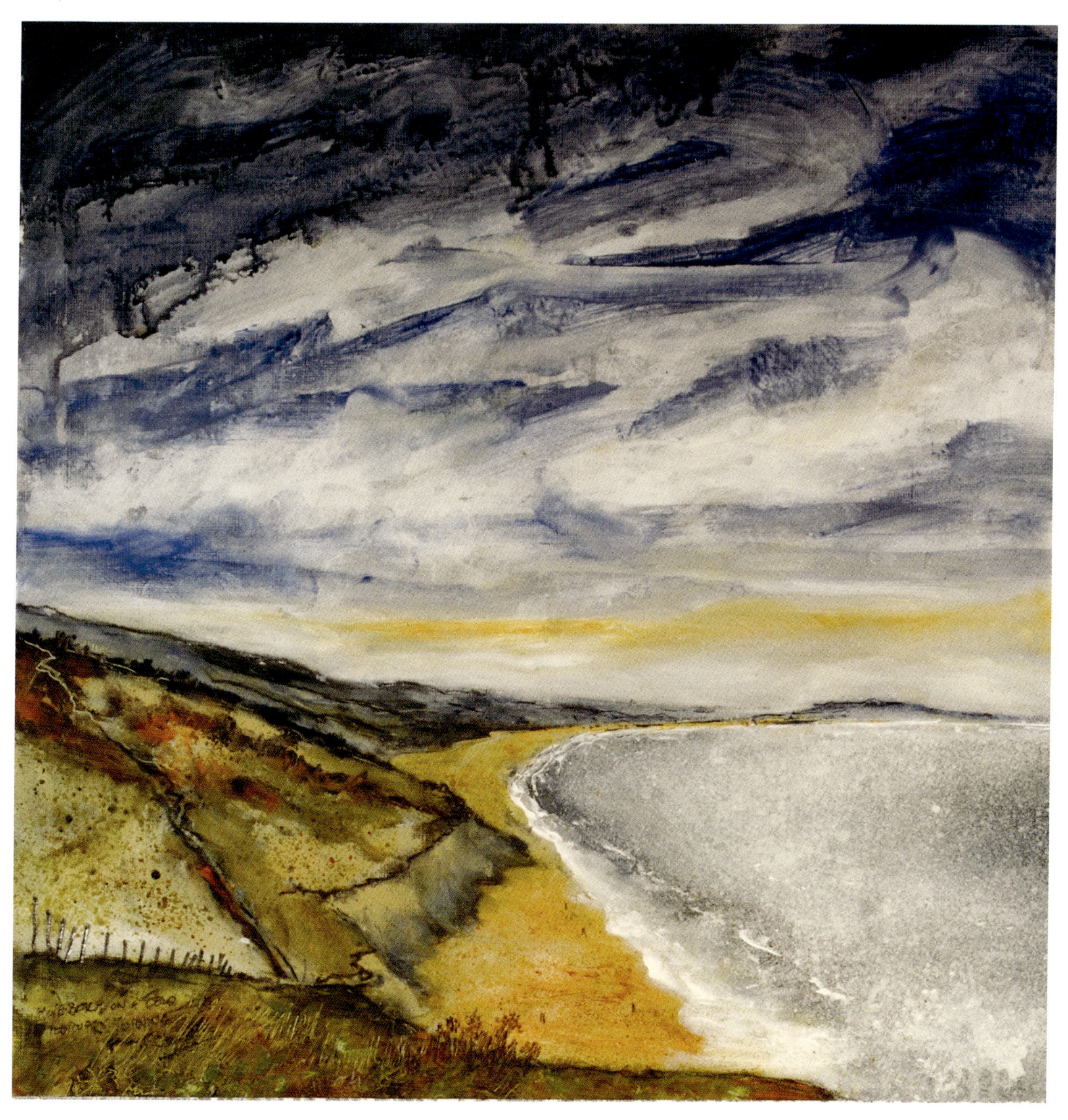

A finger stabbing the sea

Tide on schedule pounces

Rock hopping

The sea's bilges

Pumped out twice a day

Swell - a force to be reckoned with.

West Bay

Time to get off the rocks while I still can!

Mixed media
22 x 22cm

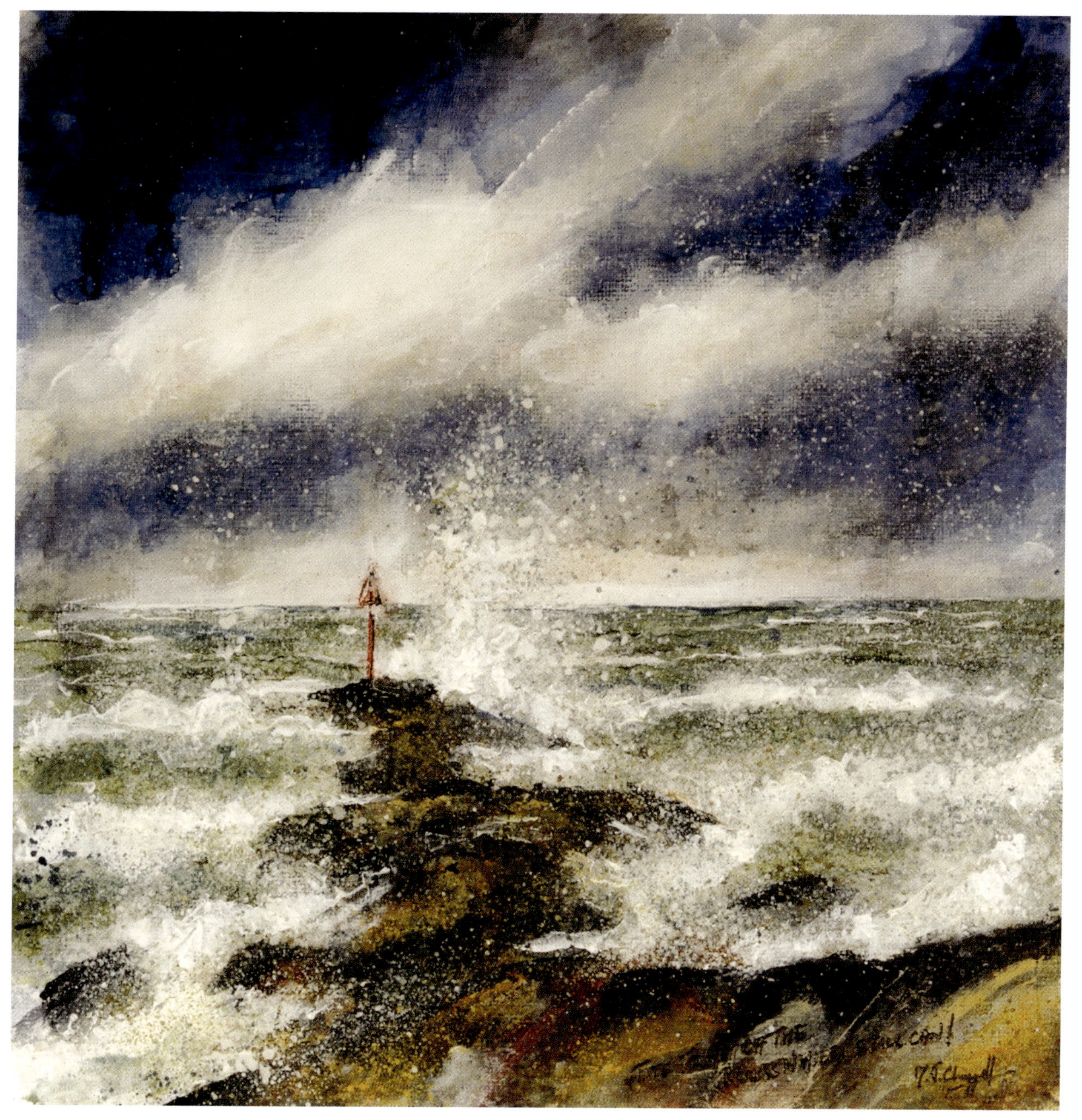

Fractured silence

The ocean sleeps

Fishing for compliments

Horizon, sharp, merges

Cutting the light

Into rashers

Undercliff faltering

On the edge, no man's land.

Raven territory - reflection calling.

The Undercliff

Only the sound of the sea, stream and seagulls break my solitude.

Mixed media
22 x 22cm

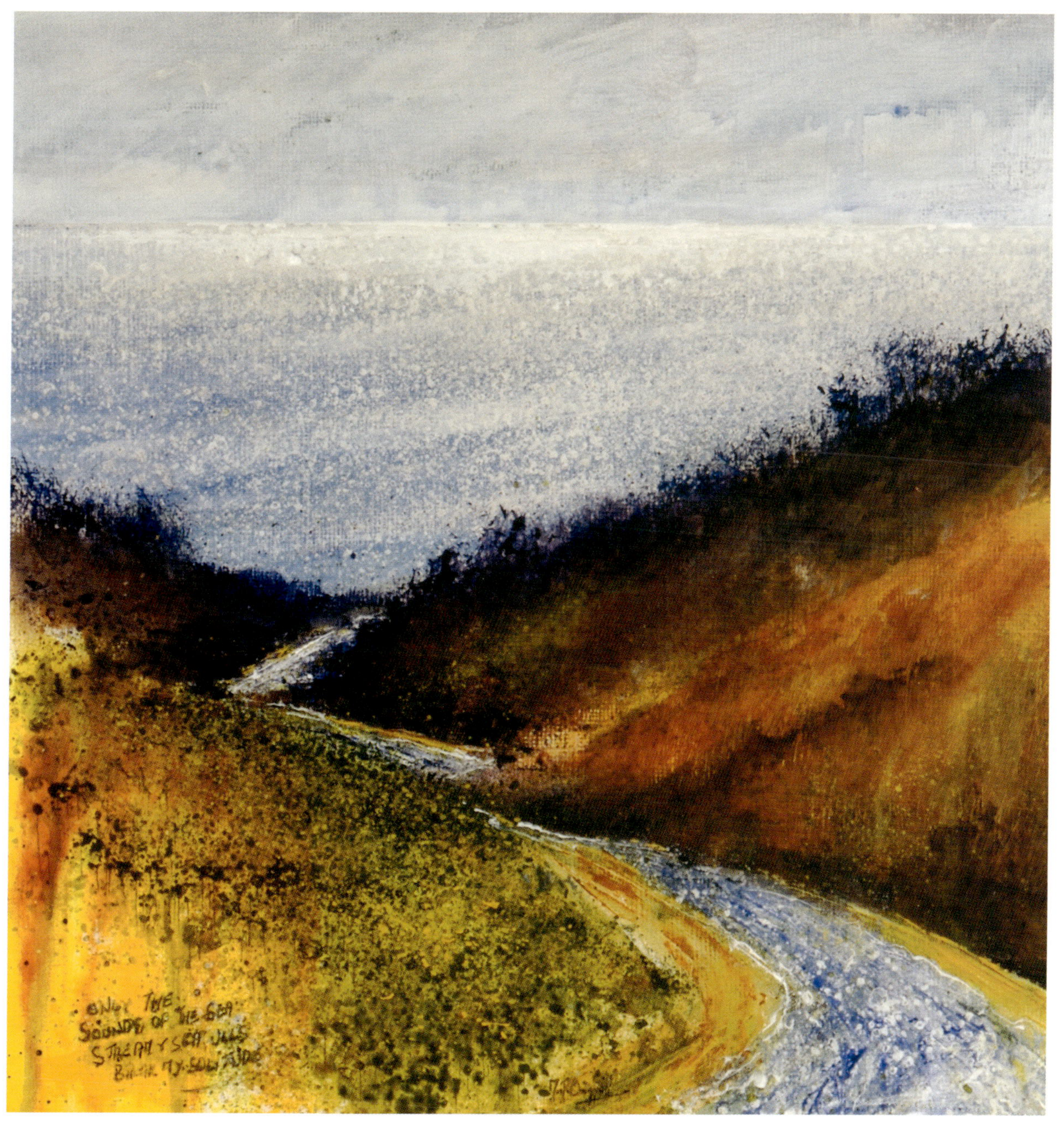
ONLY THE
SOUNDS OF THE SEA

Bound for West Bay
Inshore fishermen
Straddle the deck

Stonewalling the breakers
The sky netted
Punishing waves

Trawling the deep
The undertow tugs
At the colour of sky

Paint flakes
Tides cast adrift
Bring in their own cargo

Shelving the pots, the sea untethered.
Mad about the buoy -
The race out of control.

Bringing home the catch

Mixed media
44 x 14cm

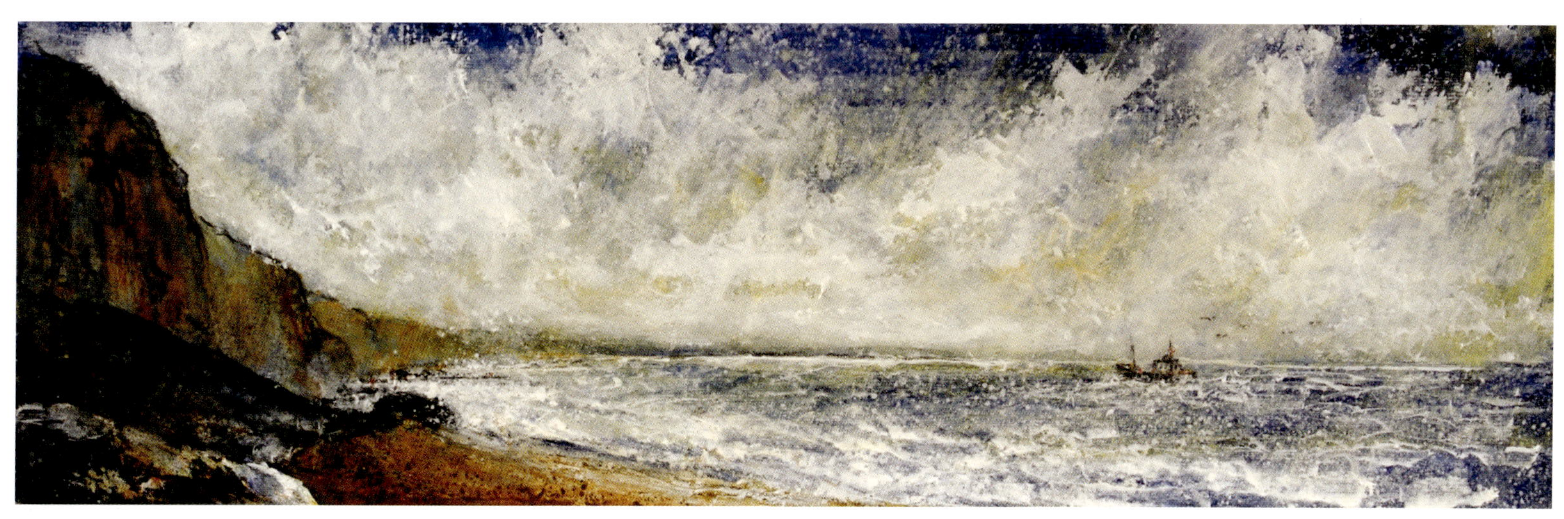

Hidden cove beneath the rock chiselling the coast
St Aldhelm's quarry sea shimmering
Round the corner Aegean light

Pulling the surface taught the sea's saga stranded
On Kimmeridge ledges lured ashore by burning cliffs
Oil wells oracles in Lulworth
Scylla and Carybdis on remand

Visiting Cyclops on Portland the myth descends
Poseidon plays around with torpedoes
Chats up sirens in Weymouth spinning the roulette wheel
Penelope is voted in the County Council.
And Odysseus in search of ice cream.

Chapman's Pool – Dorset

Mixed media
92 x 61cm

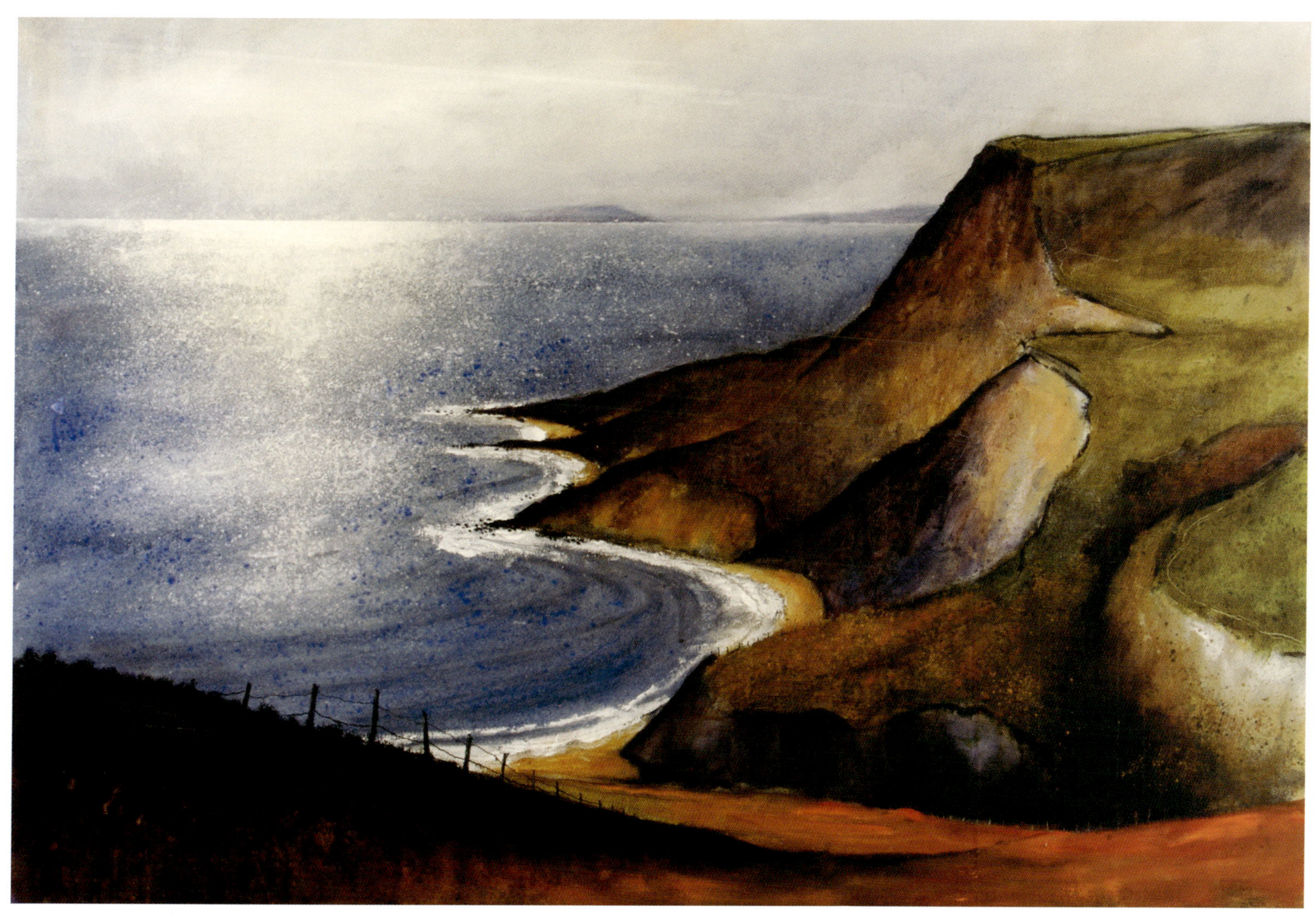

He was safe whilst still afloat in the rowing boat beyond the Cobb
But the moment he smelt sea weed the idea became reality
The undercliff beckoned him large rounded pebbles
A warning for his unsure feet all would not be well.

The Cobb in a wild winters storm from Monmouth beach

Mixed media
122 x 61cm

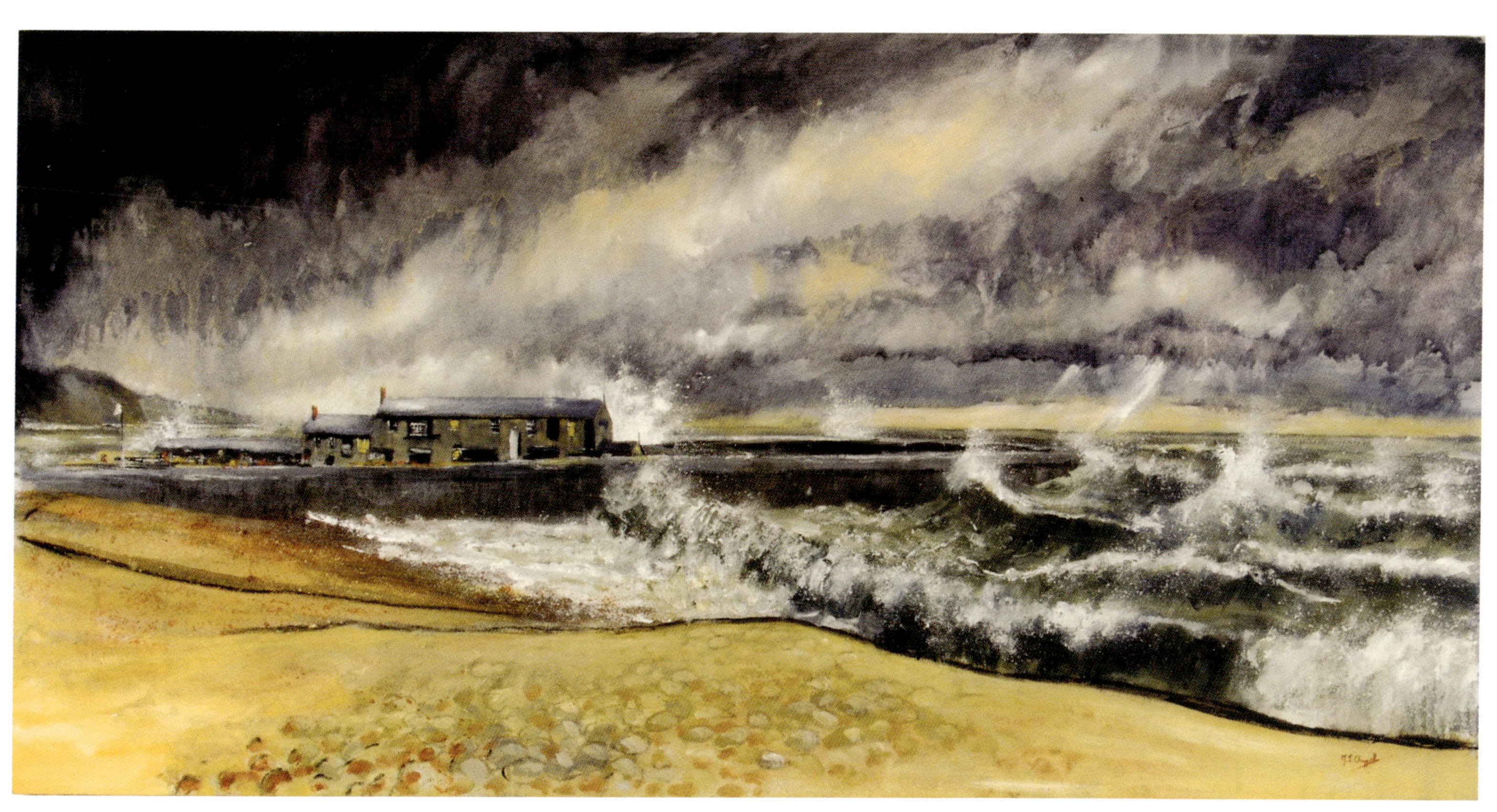

Eype Down

Shortest day of the year
Voyage of the heavens
Charted in the hedgerows

Written in the fields
Wet sky in ribbons
The turning point, an apex.

Eype Down

Winter solstice sunset

Mixed media
122 x 61cm

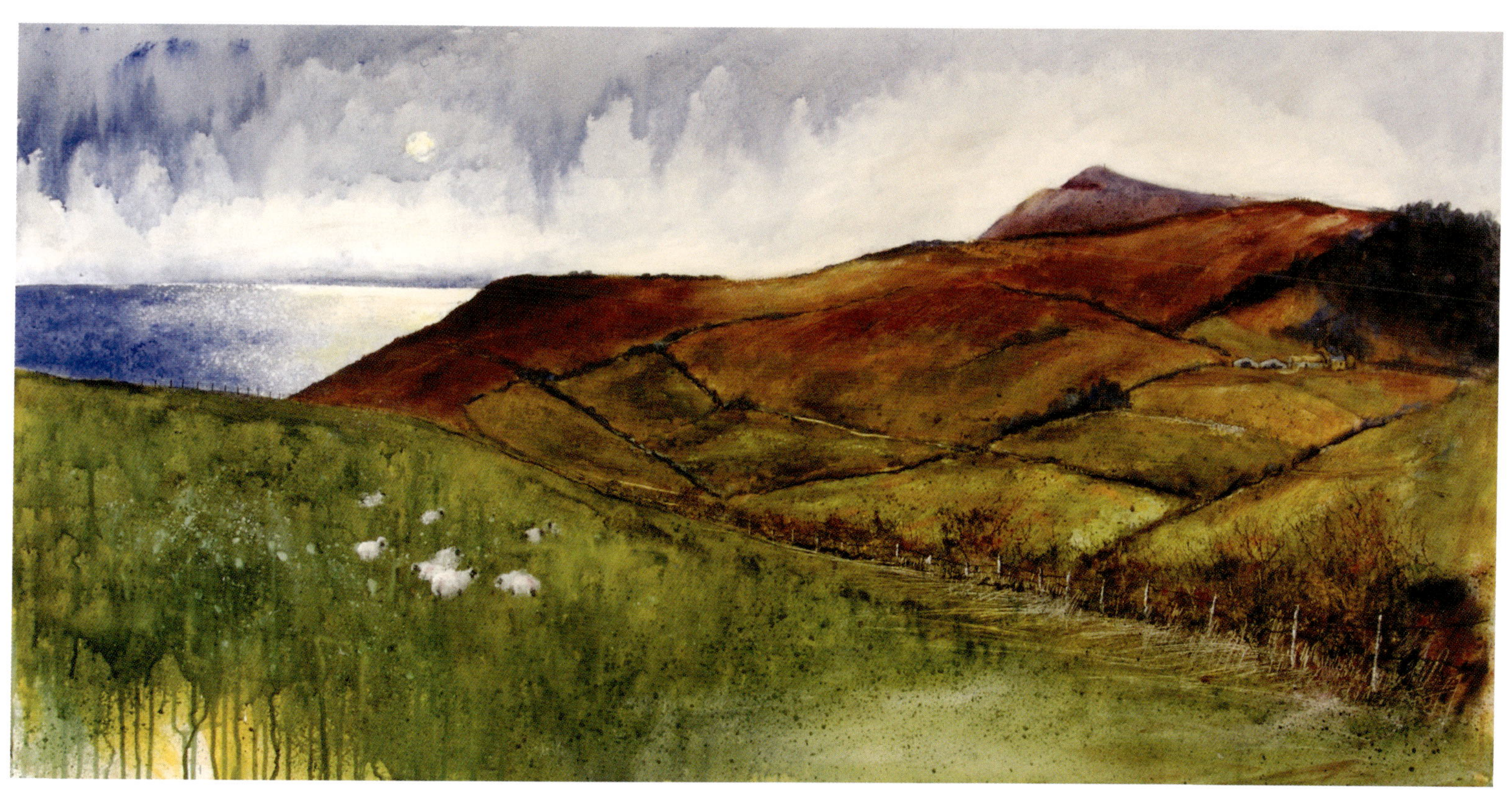

East Cliff - West Bay

South Westerly Storm

Northern light not bad for artists

Sea cliff climbing

Popular during the war

Marines destined for Normandy

Day trip with a difference

Grappling irons and life preservers

Good nesting spot for sea gulls.

Channel Pilot on hold

The beach a Zen garden

Raked by the storms.

East Cliff – West Bay

Mixed media with collage
168 x 92cm

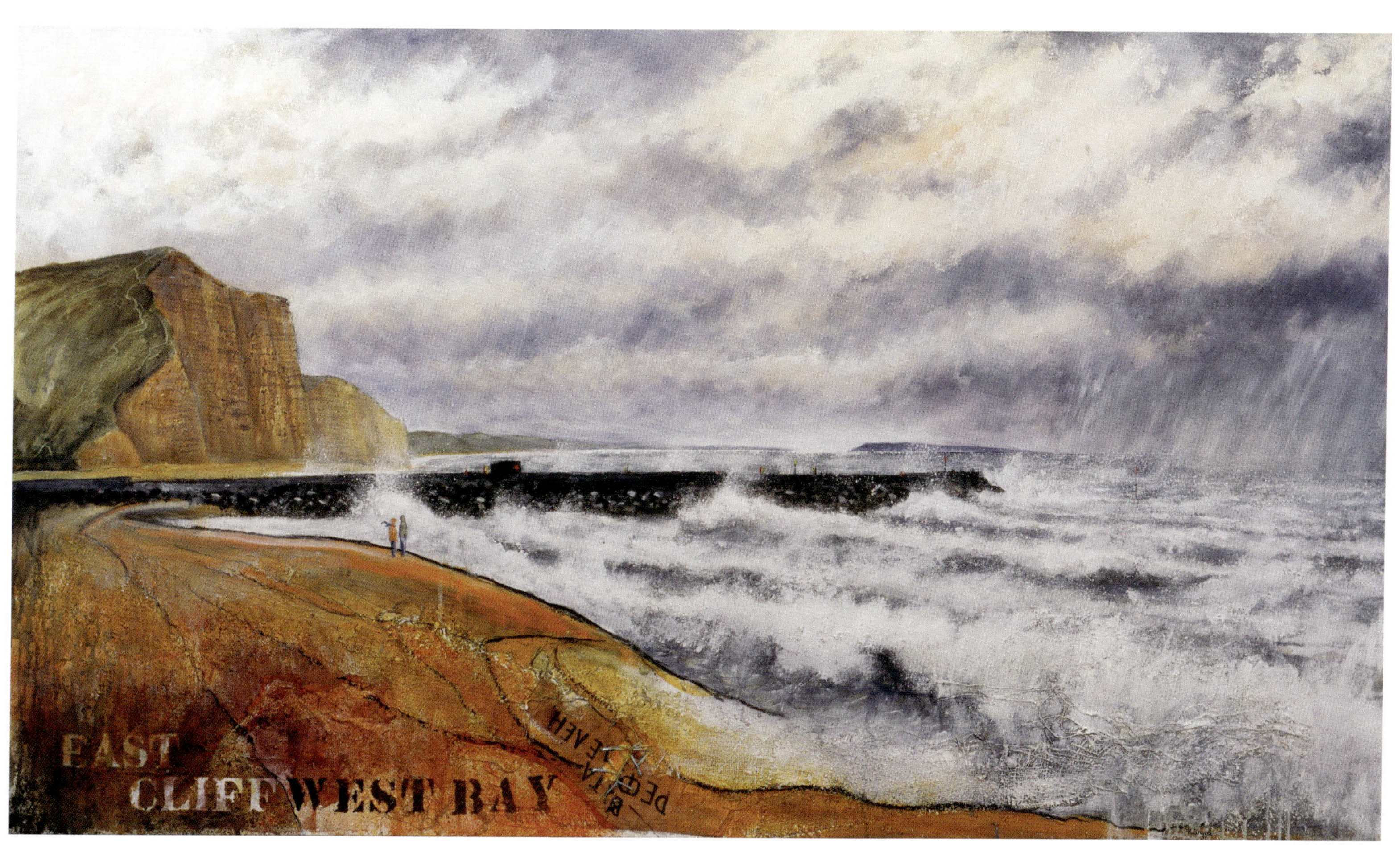
EAST
CLIFF WEST BAY

Slot machines to the right - groynes to the left
The arcade an extension of an idea
First put forward by Thomas Hollis
Who commissioned Canaletto amongst others.

The French Lieutenant's woman
Importing French sand on the side
The slippery slope of crab sandwiches and tea shops,
Crazy golf and the promenade - a shore thing.

Lyme Regis in Winter

Painted just before the bulldozers moved in!

Mixed media with collage
168 x 92cm

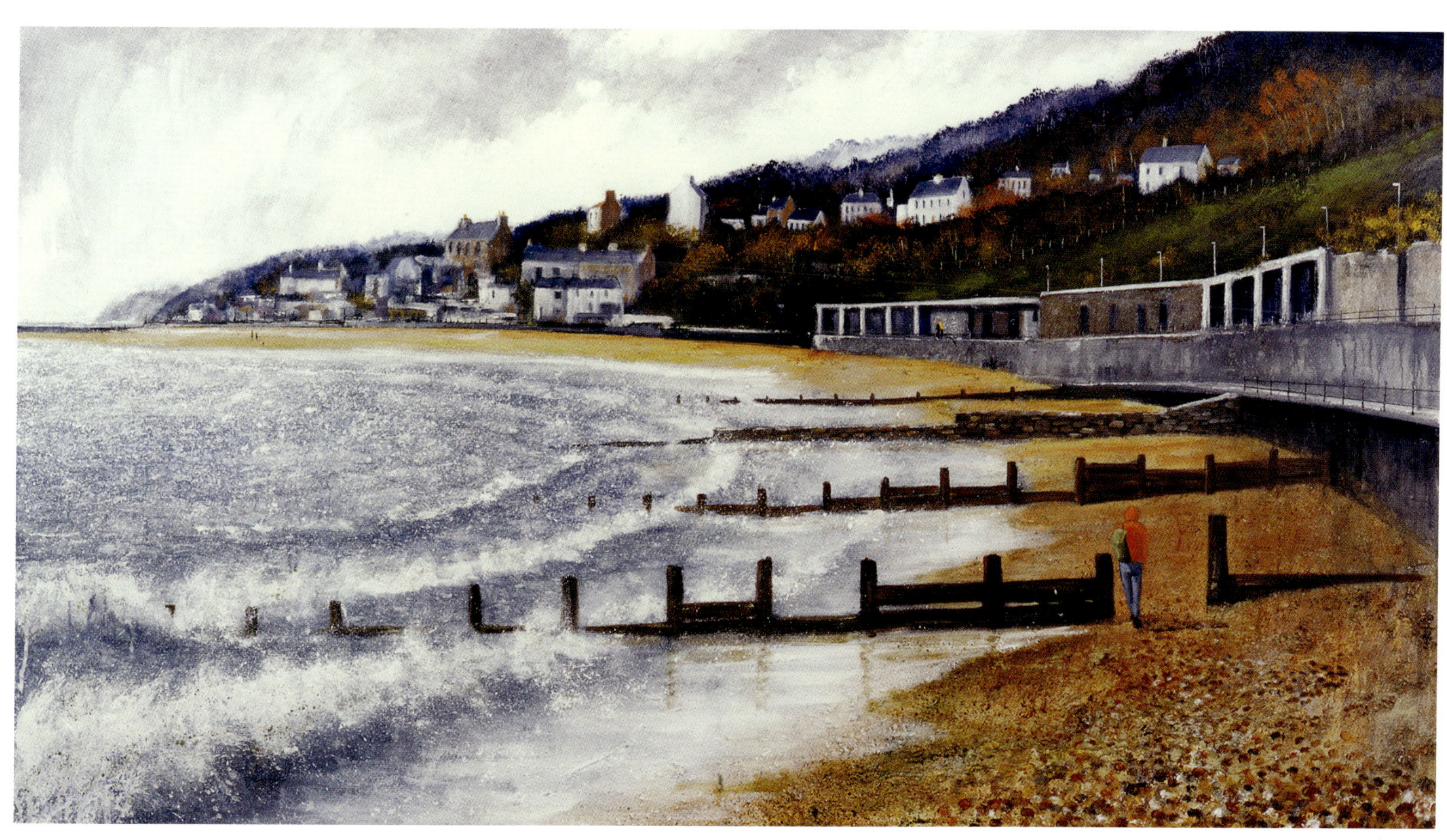

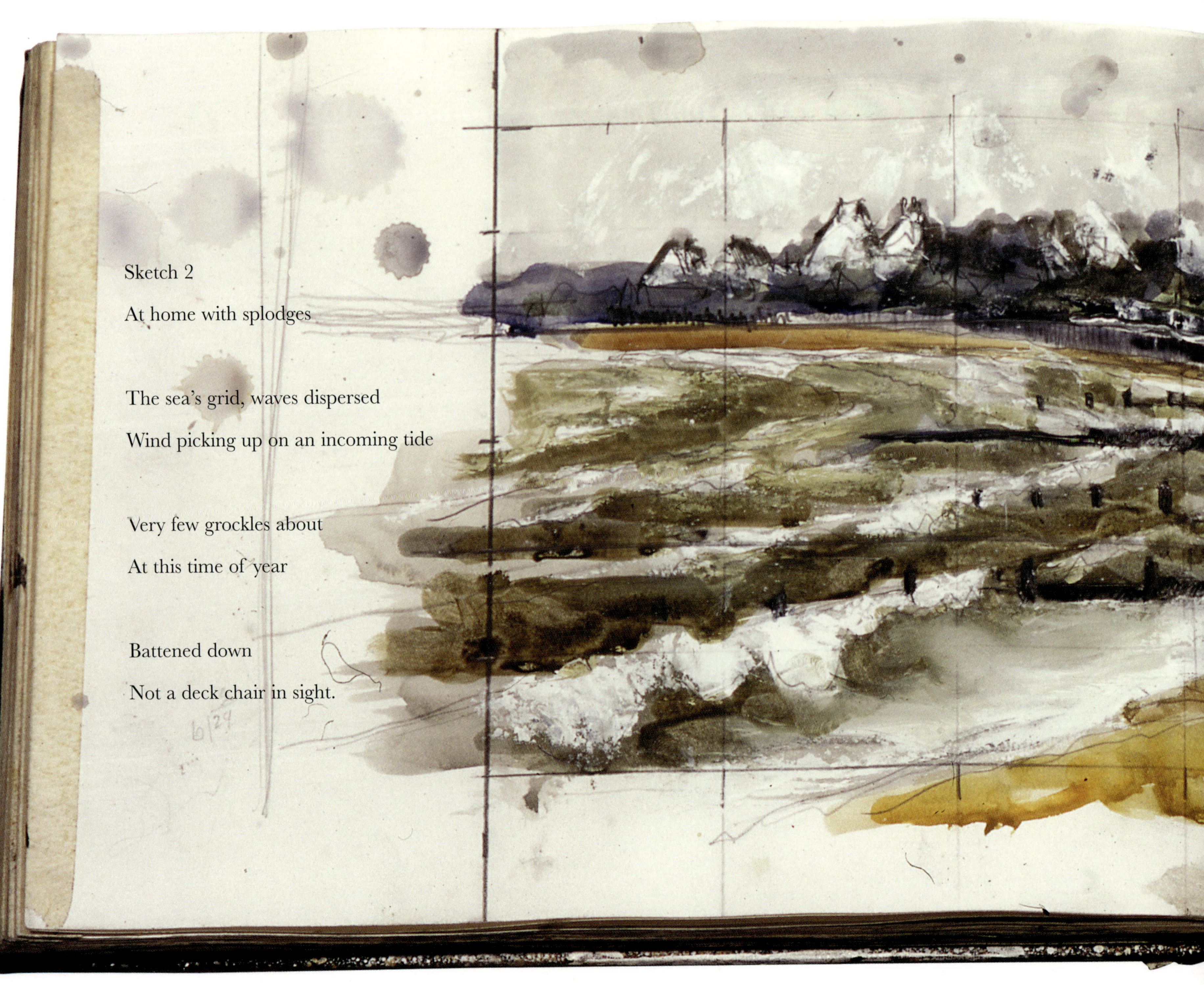

Sketch 2

At home with splodges

The sea's grid, waves dispersed
Wind picking up on an incoming tide

Very few grockles about
At this time of year

Battened down
Not a deck chair in sight.